My Community Long Ago

Bobbie Kalman

Dalmatian Press

Created by Bobbie Kalman

Published in 2013 by Dalmatian Press, LLC, Franklin, TN 37068-2068.
1-866-418-2572. DalmatianPress.com

CE16258/1012
Printed in China

Author and Editor-in-Chief
Bobbie Kalman

Reading Consultant
Elaine Hurst

Editors
Kathy Middleton
Crystal Sikkens

Photo research
Bobbie Kalman

Illustrations
Barbara Bedell: pages 1, 2, 3, 5, 7, 9 (top),
11 (top), 12, 13, (all except center), 15, 17, 19, 21, 23
Antoinette "Cookie" Bortolon: page 9 (bottom)
Bonna Rouse: pages 11 (bottom), 13 (center)

Photographs
Fotolia: page 22 (all except bottom)
other photographs by Shutterstock

What is in this book?

What is a community? 4

Family homes 6

Places to shop 8

Places to learn 10

Fun at school 12

Growing food 14

Clothes 16

Working together 18

Travel now and then 20

No machines 22

Index 24

What is a community?

A community is a place where people live and work together.

My community long ago looked different than it does today.

My community long ago was a village
with buildings, roads, and farms.
The people who lived there helped
one another in many ways.

Family homes

Today, people live in different kinds of homes.
I live in an apartment with nine rooms.
My friends and I are reading in my bedroom.

In my community long ago,
some homes had only one room.
They cooked, ate, played,
worked, and slept there.

Places to shop

I like going to the shopping mall. You can find almost anything there! I like the clothing stores and toy stores.

In my community long ago, people shopped at a general store. They brought things, such as eggs, to the store and traded them for other things, such as cloth or dishes.

Places to learn

I go to a big school with many classrooms and teachers. At school, I write my school work on paper with a pencil.

My community long ago had
one classroom and one teacher.
Children did their school work on
small chalkboards called slates.

Fun at school

How do you have fun
at school? What games
do you play at recess?
Do you play any of the
recess games that these
children played long ago?

leap frog

jump rope

dodgeball

clapping games

hide and seek

Growing food

Farmers grow food and trucks bring
the food to my community.
We buy the food at a supermarket.

In my community long ago, most people grew their own food. Schools grew vegetable gardens, too.

Clothes

I wear different
clothes every day.
On special days,
I like to dress in
my best clothes.

Most children long ago
had only two outfits.
They wore one every day
and the other on Sundays.

Boys wore pants, shirts,
and straw hats every day.
Girls wore dresses and aprons.

everyday clothes

Sunday clothes

Working together

People in my community work at jobs.
They are paid money for the work they do.
They buy the things they need with money.
This family has just bought a home.

In my community long ago, people helped one another build homes and do other big jobs. After working together, people ate, danced, played games, and had a lot of fun.

Travel now and then

In my community today, people travel by bicycle, car, subway, plane, and bus. My friends and I travel to school in a school bus.

In my community long ago, people walked, rode horses, or traveled in wagons pulled by horses. In snow, horses pulled sleighs.

No machines

Today we use many machines
to help us do work.
Name all the machines
you know that people use.

My community long ago had no machines to help them. They used tools to help make their clothes and furniture by hand.

Index

food page 14-15

fun (games) page 12-13, 19

clothes
pages 16-17, 22

stores pages 8-9

travel pages 20-21

work pages 18-19, 22

homes pages 6-7, 15, 18-19

village page 5

schools pages 10-11, 12, 15